Lohne

Food Dudes

ROBERT CADE:

Gatorade Inventor

Joanne Mattern
ABDO Publishing Company

visit us at
www.abdopublishing.com

Published by ABDO Publishing Company, 8000 West 78th Street, Edina, Minnesota 55439.
Copyright © 2011 by Abdo Consulting Group, Inc. International copyrights reserved in all
countries. No part of this book may be reproduced in any form without written permission from the
publisher. The Checkerboard Library™ is a trademark and logo of ABDO Publishing Company.

Printed in the United States of America, North Mankato, Minnesota.
092010
012011

 PRINTED ON RECYCLED PAPER

Cover Photos: AP Images
Interior Photos: Alamy pp. 19, 25; AP Images p. 1; courtesy Cade Museum for Innovation
    and Invention pp. 4, 5, 6, 7, 8, 9, 10, 11, 13, 18, 20, 21, 26, 27; courtesy Department of Special
    Collections, University of Florida Archives Photo Collection p. 15; Getty Images p. 23;
    Public Domain p. 24; courtesy University of Florida p. 17

Series Coordinator: BreAnn Rumsch
Editors: Heidi M.D. Elston, BreAnn Rumsch
Art Direction & Cover Design: Neil Klinepier

Library of Congress Cataloging-in-Publication Data

Mattern, Joanne, 1963-
  Robert Cade : Gatorade inventor / Joanne Mattern.
    p. cm. -- (Food dudes)
  ISBN 978-1-61613-556-0
  1. Cade, Robert, 1927-2007--Juvenile literature. 2. Energy drinks--United States--History--
Juvenile literature. 3. Beverage industry--United States--History--Juvenile literature. 4. Inventors--
United States--Biography--Juvenile literature. 5. Businessmen--United States--Biography--Juvenile
literature. I. Title.
  HD9348.U52C336 2011
  338.7'6636--dc22
  [B]
                                        2010027884

Contents

Texas Boy

Chances are, you have enjoyed a cold Gatorade on a hot day. Dr. Robert Cade used science to invent this famous drink. It became the first sports drink and led to an amazing business success story.

James Robert Cade was born on September 26, 1927, in San Antonio, Texas. He went by Robert. Robert was named for his father, who was a lawyer. His mother, Winifred, took care of the home. Robert grew up with a younger sister named Thelma.

From a young age, Robert proved to be a gifted musician. When he was seven, he began taking violin lessons. He also loved to sing. He often performed for his family and friends.

Robert Cade in 1945

Thelma took piano lessons. She and Robert liked performing together.

Growing up, Robert enjoyed being active. He liked to ride his bicycle and practice archery. He even worked at an archery range during the summer he was 14.

In 1933, Robert began attending Highland Park Elementary School in San Antonio. Later, he attended Page Junior High School. Robert was a good student. He was also a good athlete. He ran on the track team at Breckenridge High School.

By 1945, **World War II** was raging. That spring, Robert joined the U.S. Navy shortly before graduation. He left school to provide medical care to sailors.

Medical School

In 1948, Robert decided to leave the navy and go to college. He attended the University of Texas in Austin. There, he studied history and German. In 1950, Robert began attending Southwestern Medical School of the University of Texas in Dallas. He wanted to be a doctor.

Southwestern Medical School

During medical school, Robert met a nurse named Mary Strasburger. He began driving Mary home from work every night. They enjoyed spending time together. Soon, they realized they were in love.

In June 1953, Robert and Mary married. Over the next few years, they had six children. They named them Michael, Martha, Celia, Stephen, Emily, and Phoebe.

Robert graduated from medical school in 1954. He still had much studying to do before he could practice medicine. He did this by working in several different hospitals. The family moved often, following Robert from job to job.

To finish his training, Robert moved to New York City, New York. He completed a **fellowship** in **physiology** at the New York Hospital-Cornell Medical Center. Finally, he could begin working

Robert loved being a husband and a father.

as a doctor! In July 1961, the family moved to Gainesville, Florida. Robert was about to begin a job there that would change his life.

Florida Gators

Cade's new job was at the University of Florida (UF). He worked as a professor of medicine. Cade also worked as the doctor for the UF football team, the Gators. In August 1965, the team was in bad shape. Cade treated 25 players for **dehydration** and **heatstroke** in one weekend.

Soon after, Dwayne Douglas came to see Cade. Douglas was an assistant coach for the **freshman** football team. His players never had to go to the bathroom after a game. He wanted to know why. This turned out to be a very important question.

Cade was a popular teacher at the University of Florida.

Cade thought he knew the answer. Florida's extreme heat caused players to sweat. They sweat so much that their bodies had no water left to make **urine**. Cade decided he needed to find a way to help the Gators. So, he began studying the science of sweat.

Cade enjoyed using science to solve problems.

Sweat Test

Cade (far right) *worked with Alejandro Quesada, Jim Free, and Dana Shires* (left to right) *to help the Gators.*

Cade knew that sweat contains water and salt. Replacing just water or just salt was not the solution for the football players. Drinking too much water gave players stomach **cramps**. And, taking salt pills gave them leg cramps.

Several other doctors joined Cade to help solve this problem. They were Alejandro Quesada, Jim Free, and Dana Shires. They asked Gators head coach Ray Graves if they could study the football team.

Graves agreed to let them run tests on the **freshman** players. Cade collected blood, **urine**, and sweat samples from several players. Then, the doctors studied and measured these samples.

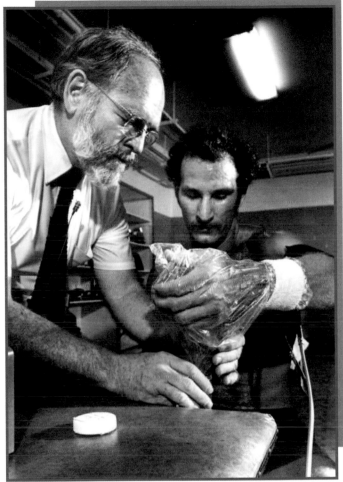

Cade collected sweat from plastic he had the players wear over their arms.

The doctors were surprised by the test results. They learned that a player could lose up to 18 pounds (8 kg) during a game. Almost all of that weight loss was water! Players could also lose up to 25 percent of their body's salt during practice.

Bad Taste, Great Name

The test results alarmed Cade. Losing so much water and salt was very dangerous. Cade was more determined than ever to help the Gators.

Cade realized a mixture of water, salt, and sugar was the answer to his problem. The body could absorb this mixture quickly. It would not sit in the stomach the way plain water did. So, it would not cause stomach **cramps** during activity.

Cade mixed water, sugar, and salt with **phosphate**. Unfortunately, the mixture tasted awful. The first time Cade drank it, he threw up! Cade's wife, Mary, suggested adding lemon juice to the mixture. This made it taste better.

At first, the doctors called the drink Cade's Cola. Then Dr. Free suggested the name Gatorade, after the football team. Everyone liked that idea, and the name stuck.

Cade created the Gatorade mixture in his lab. He knew it would help the football players stay hydrated.

The Big Gamble

Now, Cade needed to find out if his formula worked. Cade asked Coach Graves if he could test Gatorade on the football players. Graves said Cade could test it on the **freshman** football team. He did not want to risk the **varsity** players getting sick!

In October 1965, Florida's freshman football team played against the B team. Since the players on the B team were older, everyone expected them to win.

During the game, the B team drank water. The freshman team drank Gatorade. It replaced the water and salt they lost when they sweat. The B team took the lead early in the game. But everything changed in the second half. The B team became **dehydrated** while the freshmen still had energy to play well. The freshmen won the game!

Coach Graves was impressed by these results. He asked Cade to make up a huge batch of Gatorade for the varsity team. They had a big game the next day against the Louisiana State University Tigers.

Everyone expected the Gators to lose their game. But throughout it, the Gators drank Gatorade. This kept them **hydrated**. The Gators won the game in the second half! Coach Graves was thrilled. He told Cade he wanted Gatorade available at every game.

*Gators head coach
Ray Graves*

Gatorade Fame

For the UF Gators, the 1965–1966 season was a great one. They finished with a record of eight wins and only two losses. Sportswriters noticed how the team played well during a game's second half. They began giving Gatorade credit for this success.

It didn't take long for word about Gatorade to spread. In November 1966, a writer from the *Miami Herald* interviewed Coach Graves and Dr. Cade. He wrote an article about Gatorade that was printed in newspapers around the world. Cade was thrilled. He said, "Our stuff was on the way."

After their winning season, the Gators played in the Orange Bowl. They played against the Georgia Institute of Technology Yellow Jackets. The game was held in Miami Gardens, Florida.

The Gators won the game! Afterward, Yellow Jackets coach Bobby Dodd spoke with Coach Graves. He said, "We didn't have Gatorade. That made the difference."

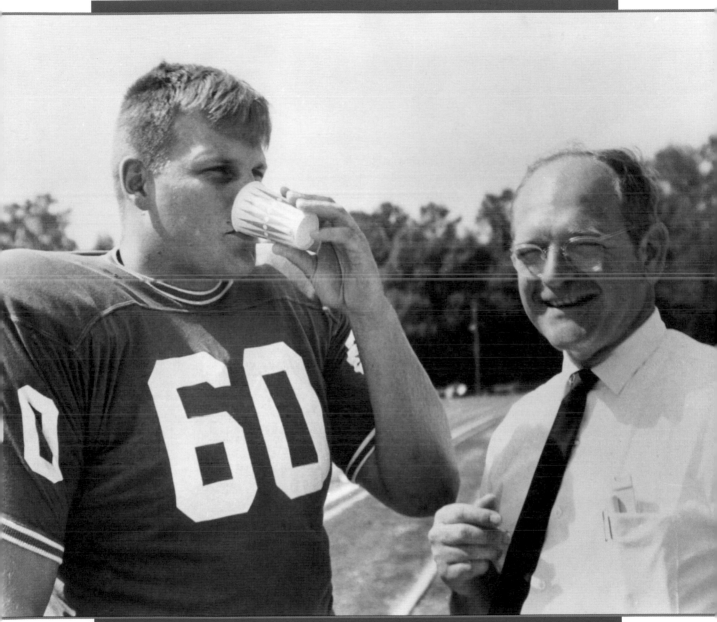

The performance of the football players proved that Gatorade worked.

Gatorade was originally sold in cans, but the salt in the mixture rusted them! Then, Stokely switched to glass bottles.

It wasn't long before other teams wanted Gatorade. Cade believed he could make a lot of money selling the drink. But first, he needed money to produce it. Cade went to UF officials. He asked them for $10,000 so he could keep making Gatorade. He even offered to sell the drink to the school. But the university said no.

Luckily, a food company named Stokely-Van Camp was interested in buying Gatorade. Cade and the other doctors prepared to sell. In March 1967, they **incorporated** Gatorade Inc. By the next month, they legally owned the name Gatorade.

In May, the doctors sold the Gatorade name and recipe to Stokely-Van Camp. In return, Stokely agreed to give them each a percentage of Gatorade's sales.

Stokely-Van Camp worked to improve the taste of Gatorade. They made it sweeter and created more flavors. They began selling Gatorade to sports teams in July 1967. That year, it became the official sports drink of the National Football League (NFL).

In 1968, Gatorade appeared on grocery store shelves around the United States. Now anyone could buy it! Stokely-Van Camp advertised Gatorade as the Big Thirst Quencher.

Today's plastic Gatorade bottles provide consumers with a convenient way to carry around their Gatorade.

Legal Troubles

Cade was happy with Gatorade's success. However, the drink's popularity caused him problems with the U.S. government and the University of Florida.

As a doctor at UF, the National Institute of Health gave Cade grant money. This money was meant to help him conduct medical research at the university.

In early 1967, the U.S. government learned that Cade had used some of this money for other purposes. In 1965, he had used

$42 to help create Gatorade. The government agreed to settle this problem. All Cade had to do was reveal what was in Gatorade. Cade promised to publish his research and formula.

The money Gatorade brings in has helped pay for many projects in the University of Florida's School of Medicine.

The Independent Florida Alligator, Tuesday, November 20, 1973, Page 5

Cade's Gatorade rakes in royalties

By PAUL RAMSEY
Alligator Staff Writer

"Say coach, you look like you could use some Gatorade," the exhausted football player said. This fictitious situation orginates in a popular television commercial on a hot and dry practice field where at least one player needs a thirst quencher.

But what is more fact than fiction is the sale of Gatorade thirst quencher has brought $115,296 to UF during the first year of a royalty agreement that ended Sept. 1.

GATORADE IS marketed nationwide by Stokely-Van Camp.

Gatorade, developed at UF in Sept. 1965, was the result of research conducted by Dr. James Robert Cade, a professor in the College of Medicine. Cade and a team of post doctoral research fellows were studying salt and water loss in the body.

Except for a few thousand dollars, most of the money received in 1972-73 has not been spent. The money is earmarked for research and general studies at the College of Medicine. Dr. Harold P. Hanson, university vice president, will recommend $75,000 be spent this year.

ONE OF the world's outstanding kidney and renal specialists, Dr. Robert F. Pitts, has plans for research work at UF. He is currently a professor of physiology at Cornell University.

Hanson said UF will use the money to help support his program when he gets here." Dr. Pitts plans to retire from his post at Cornell to come here in July, 1974, to continue his work in kidney metabolism.

About $30,000 can be spent on equipment, supplies and the salaries of post doctoral fellows before Pitts arrives.

ACCORDING TO Hanson, UF's cut was $4,000 more this July than last July, and royalties are expected to increase. A $2 million promotional campaign launched by Stokely-Van Camp may also boost the sale of Gatorade and the royalties.

The drink was first used by UF's Gator football team in 1965. One member of the post doctoral fellows team who worked on the Gatorade project later brought the drink to the attention of a representative of Stokely-Van Camp in Indiana.

Gatorade Trust, made up of researchers originally involved in the development and use of Gatorade, now earns about five cents on every gallon of Gatorade sold.

UF'S SHARE is 20 per cent of the total royalties, compensation for Dr. Cade's use of university funds and facilities in the original research. This type of revenue is relatively new to UF.

Gatorade was not the first success of Cade's research. Other drinks have been developed as a result of similar post doctoral research. Cade also holds membership in trusts for Gator Go, a high protein milk drink, and Hoppin' Gator, an alcoholic beverage.

Cade is now working on a project with another group of post doctoral fellows that has produced a high protein orange juice. His business manager is in the midst of negotiations and anticipates a contract with either Nabisco or Nestle's.

DR. ROBERT CADE
...currently working on new orange juice

Meanwhile, UF discovered Gatorade was earning Cade a lot of money. The school believed it owned Gatorade since the drink was invented there. School officials wanted Cade to give them all the profits.

Cade refused to give the money to the school. So by 1971, UF filed a lawsuit against Cade and the other doctors. Finally in July 1972, the doctors agreed to give the school 20 percent of Gatorade's total earnings.

Gatorade Splash

In 1983, the Quaker Oats Company bought Stokely-Van Camp. Two years later, Quaker asked basketball star Michael Jordan to appear in commercials for Gatorade. But Jordan asked for more money than Quaker could pay.

That same year, Gatorade got a special kind of advertising. In October, the New York Giants of the NFL won a big game. To celebrate, some players poured a bucket of Gatorade over their coach, Bill Parcells. They did the same thing the next week.

Soon, other teams began pouring Gatorade on their coaches after big wins. Fans loved these Gatorade showers! Today, this wet tradition continues.

In 1991, Quaker once again asked Jordan to appear in Gatorade commercials. This time, he agreed to represent the drink. Advertisements showed Jordan drinking Gatorade. They encouraged people to "Be Like Mike." The commercials were very successful. Now, even more people wanted to drink Gatorade.

During the 1990s, Michael Jordan was one of the world's most famous athletes.

Important Work

By 1988, Gatorade had become respected in the sports community. That year, Quaker had opened the Gatorade Sports Science Institute (GSSI) in Barrington, Illinois. Athletes travel there to determine their **hydration** and **nutrition** needs. This information helps them perform better.

GSSI works with scientists around the world. They research exercise and nutrition.

Gatorade did not just help athletes. It was also used to help ill and **dehydrated** children around the world. Cade was proud that Gatorade had saved many lives.

In the early 1990s, Cade invented a drink called TQ2. TQ2 stands for Thirst Quencher Two. Cade claimed it worked even better than Gatorade. In 1993, Quaker bought the rights to TQ2. However, it never manufactured the product.

Athletes from NFL players to kids on school sports teams drink Gatorade to stay hydrated.

Pepsico bought Quaker in 2000. It made Gatorade an even more successful product. Today, Gatorade is the most popular sports drink in the world.

Cade continued to work at the University of Florida until he retired in November 2004. There, he researched how diet affects children with **autism**. He also applied this research to help people with mental illness.

Helpful Inventor

Gatorade had made Cade a wealthy man. Yet, he never stopped working hard to help people. Cade invented a new football helmet that gave players better protection. He also invented devices to help victims of **polio**.

In his free time, Cade enjoyed many other activities. He was an accomplished writer and poet. He continued to play the violin. He also collected violins and old cars.

The Cades

Cade and his wife believed strongly in helping others. So together, they established the Gloria Dei Foundation. This organization works to help families in need.

By 2007, Cade suffered from kidney disease. That April, the University of Florida added him to their Athletic Hall of Fame. Then on November 27, Robert Cade died in Gainesville, Florida.

Cade created the most popular sports drink in the world. He used science to create a way for athletes to stay healthy in extreme conditions. Thanks to Gatorade, people today can be as active as they want. Cade's contribution will be remembered every time someone reaches for this important drink.

Helping other people remained important to Cade throughout his life.

Timeline

1927 On September 26, James Robert Cade was born in San Antonio, Texas.

1953 In June, Robert married Mary Strasburger.

1954 Robert graduated from Southwestern Medical School of the University of Texas in Dallas.

1965 In August, Cade began studying the science of sweat; by October, he was ready to test Gatorade on the University of Florida Gators football team.

1967 In March, Cade and his associates incorporated Gatorade Inc.; in May, they sold Gatorade to Stokely-Van Camp.

1972 Cade and his associates agreed to give the University of Florida 20 percent of Gatorade's earnings.

1983 The Quaker Oats Company bought Stokely-Van Camp; the first Gatorade shower took place.

1988 Quaker opened the Gatorade Sports Science Institute in Barrington, Illinois.

2000 Pepsico bought Quaker.

2004 Cade retired from the University of Florida in November.

2007 In April, the University of Florida added Cade to their Athletic Hall of Fame; on November 27, Robert Cade died in Gainesville, Florida.

Liquid Fuel

Gatorade is an important sports drink to many types of professional athletes. Even race car drivers depend on Gatorade.

For many years, race car drivers did not stay hydrated enough while racing. Races can last for hours. During that time, drivers sweat large amounts.

In 2001, GSSI and Gatorade went to work developing the Gatorade In-Car Drinking System (GIDS). It provides the driver with a hands-free way to drink Gatorade during a race. This system keeps drivers fueled and focused to win. Today, the GIDS is considered a vital piece of racing equipment.

Famous drivers known to rely on the GIDS include Jimmie Johnson, Ryan Newman, and Matt Kenseth.

Glossary

autism - a developmental disorder that affects communication and social relationships.

cramp - a sharp, painful tightening that occurs suddenly in a muscle or a group of muscles.

dehydration - the loss or removal of water. When lost or used water is not replaced, a person becomes dehydrated.

fellowship - the position of a person appointed for advanced study or research.

freshman - a first-year student.

heatstroke - a condition marked by a lack of sweating, high body temperature, and fainting. It is caused by extended exposure to high temperatures.

hydrate - to supply with ample liquid or moisture.

incorporate - to form into a legal corporation.

nutrition - that which promotes growth, provides energy, repairs body tissues, and maintains life.

phosphate (FAHS-fayt) - an organic compound that aids in the release of energy.

physiology (fih-zee-AH-luh-jee) - a branch of biology dealing with the normal functions of living things. A physiologist studies the processes and activities by which life is carried on.

polio - the common name for poliomyelitis. This disease usually affects children and sometimes leaves people paralyzed.

urine - waste material produced by the kidneys. In mammals, urine is usually a yellowish liquid.

varsity - the main team that represents a school in athletic or other competition.

World War II - from 1939 to 1945, fought in Europe, Asia, and Africa. Great Britain, France, the United States, the Soviet Union, and their allies were on one side. Germany, Italy, Japan, and their allies were on the other side.

Web Sites

To learn more about Robert Cade, visit ABDO Publishing Company online. Web sites about Robert Cade are featured on our Book Links page. These links are routinely monitored and updated to provide the most current information available.

www.abdopublishing.com

Index